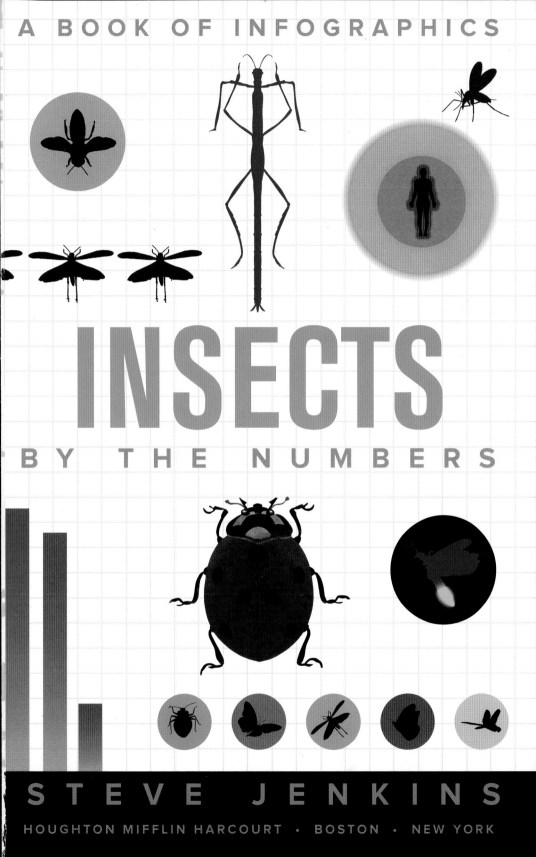

A BOOK OF INFOGRAPHICS

# INSECTS

## BY THE NUMBERS

STEVE JENKINS

HOUGHTON MIFFLIN HARCOURT · BOSTON · NEW YORK

# Contents

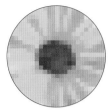

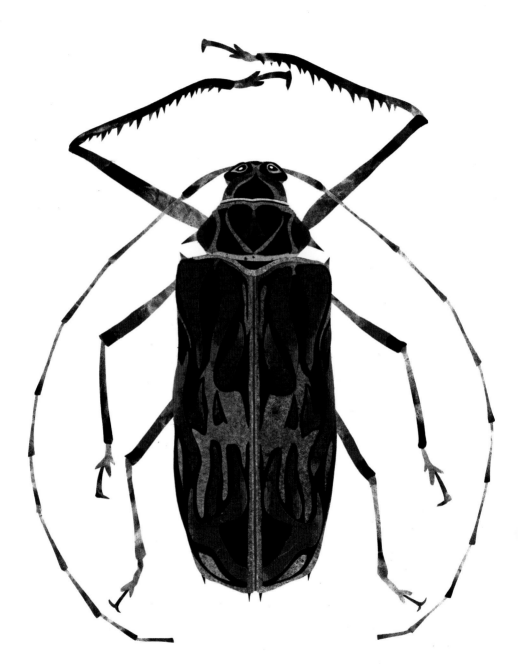

Insects are, by far, the most common kind of animal on Earth. They have been here for hundreds of millions of years, and they'll probably be here long after we are gone. Insects come in an amazing range of colors, shapes, sizes, and abilities. Most are harmless to humans, but a few can be deadly. In fact, the most dangerous animal on Earth is an insect.

The infographics in this book—maps, graphs, and diagrams—help us explore the fascinating world of these six-legged creatures.

*Words in blue can be found in the glossary on page 38.*

# What is an insect?

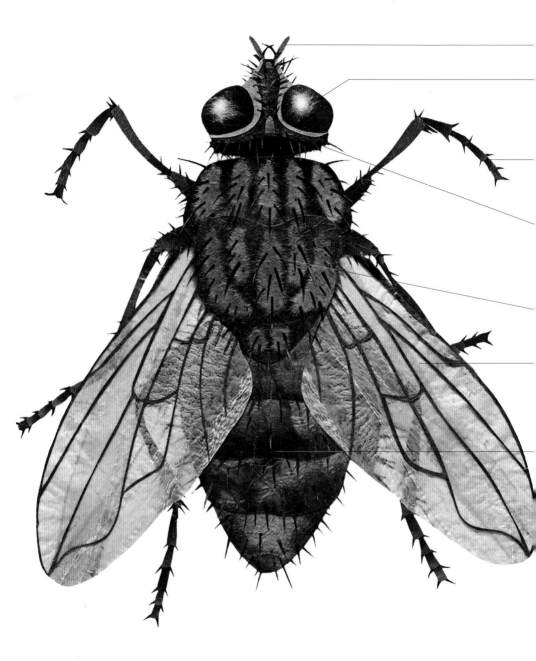

Actual size of a housefly

6

## Insect parts

Insects have two antennae . . .

two compound eyes, each with many tiny lenses . . .

six legs . . .

and three body parts.

head

thorax

abdomen

Most insects have wings.

**Insects are members of a large group of animals called arthropods.**
(These animals are all arthropods.)

insects     spiders     shrimp     crabs     lobsters    scorpions   centipedes

Arthropods have a hard outer covering instead of bones. They have bodies that are divided into segments. And they have lots of legs.

# How many insects?

There are almost 1,400,000 named species of animals. Most of them are insects.

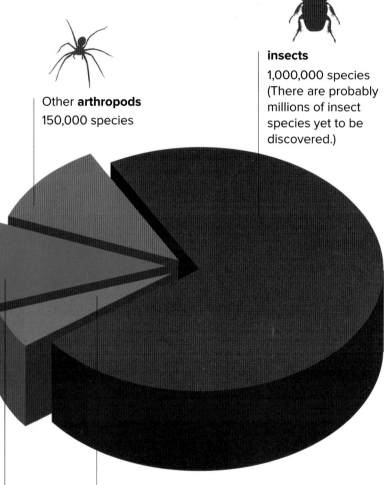

**Other arthropods**
150,000 species

**insects**
1,000,000 species
(There are probably millions of insect species yet to be discovered.)

**Other invertebrates**
(animals without a backbone)
154,000 species

**vertebrates**
(animals with a backbone: including fish, birds, reptiles, amphibians, and mammals)
63,000 species

= one pound (454 grams) of insects

= one pound (454 grams) of humans

For every pound (454 grams) of human on Earth, there are an estimated 300 pounds (136 kilograms) of insects.

# Insects large and small

These insects are shown at actual size.

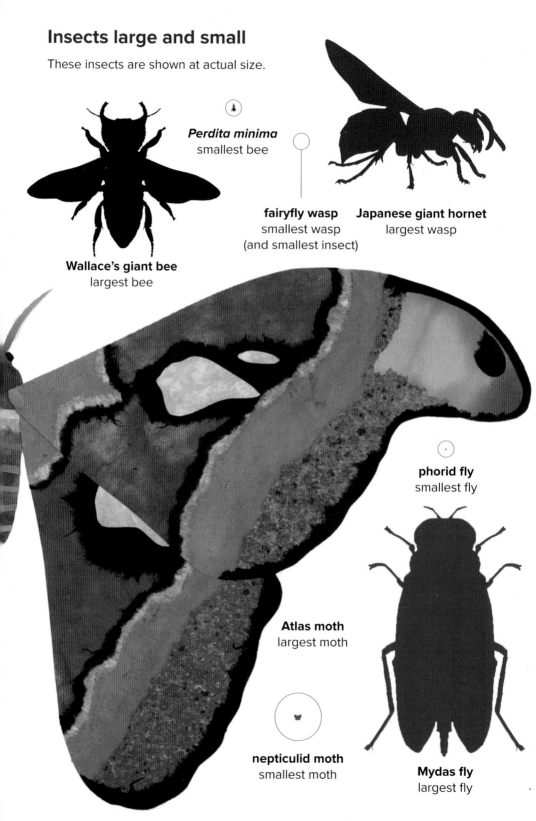

*Perdita minima*
smallest bee

**fairyfly wasp**
smallest wasp
(and smallest insect)

**Japanese giant hornet**
largest wasp

**Wallace's giant bee**
largest bee

**phorid fly**
smallest fly

**Atlas moth**
largest moth

**nepticulid moth**
smallest moth

**Mydas fly**
largest fly

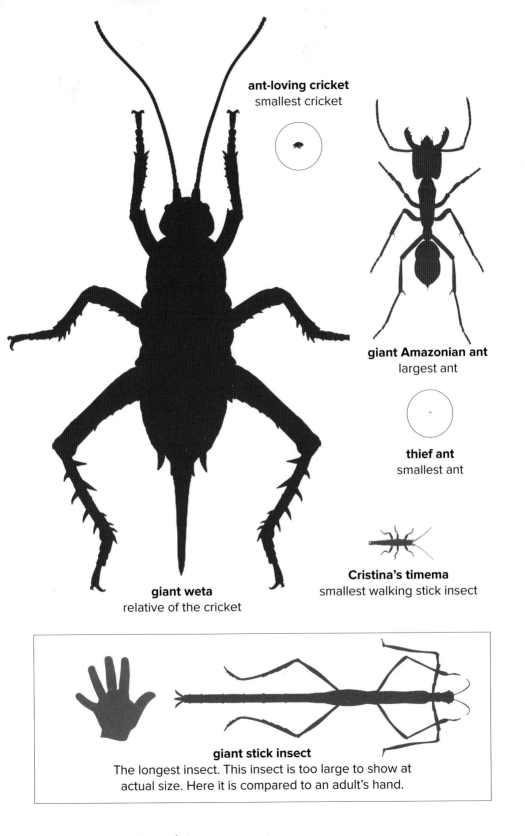

**ant-loving cricket**
smallest cricket

**giant Amazonian ant**
largest ant

**thief ant**
smallest ant

**Cristina's timema**
smallest walking stick insect

**giant weta**
relative of the cricket

**giant stick insect**
The longest insect. This insect is too large to show at
actual size. Here it is compared to an adult's hand.

# Meet the beetles

There are more beetles than any other kind of insect. In fact, almost one out of every four animals on Earth is a beetle.

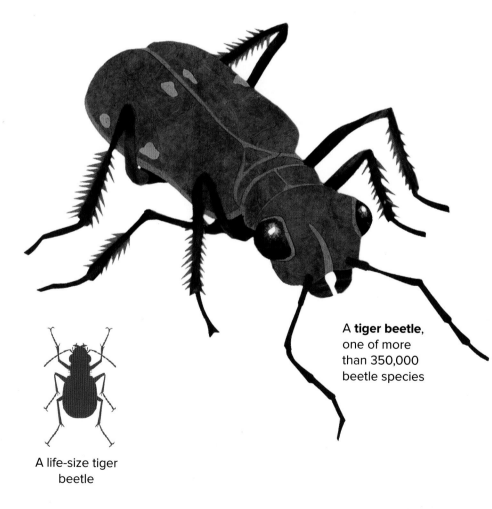

A **tiger beetle**, one of more than 350,000 beetle species

A life-size tiger beetle

Beetles come in many different shapes and sizes. These beetles are shown life-size.

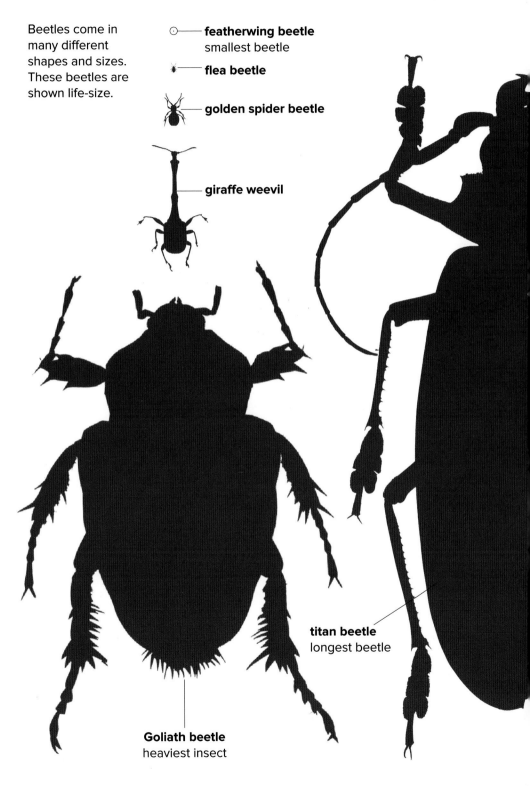

**featherwing beetle**
smallest beetle

**flea beetle**

**golden spider beetle**

**giraffe weevil**

**titan beetle**
longest beetle

**Goliath beetle**
heaviest insect

# Insect flight

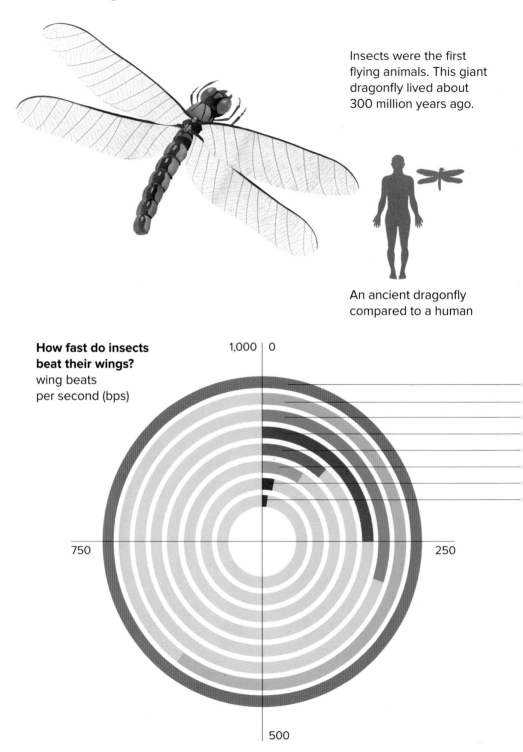

Insects were the first flying animals. This giant dragonfly lived about 300 million years ago.

An ancient dragonfly compared to a human

**How fast do insects beat their wings?**
wing beats per second (bps)

1,000 | 0

750

250

500

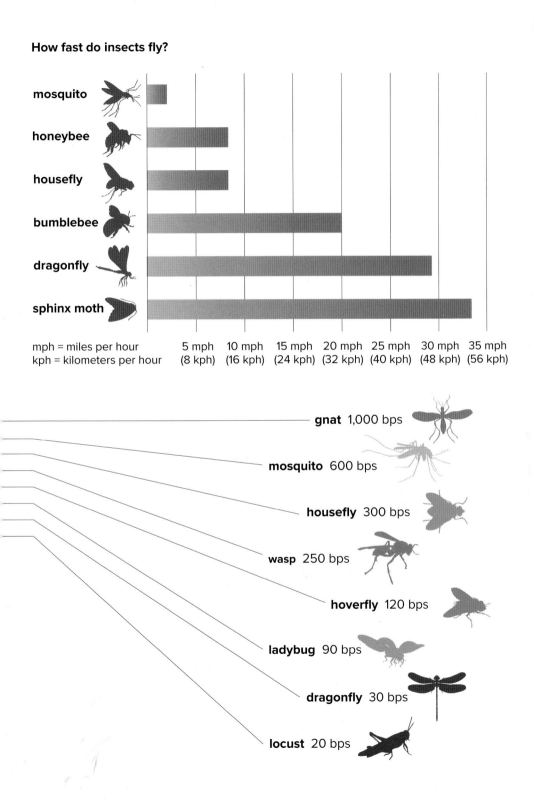

**How fast do insects fly?**

| | mph | kph |
|---|---|---|
| mosquito | | |
| honeybee | | |
| housefly | | |
| bumblebee | | |
| dragonfly | | |
| sphinx moth | | |

mph = miles per hour
kph = kilometers per hour

5 mph (8 kph)  10 mph (16 kph)  15 mph (24 kph)  20 mph (32 kph)  25 mph (40 kph)  30 mph (48 kph)  35 mph (56 kph)

**gnat** 1,000 bps

**mosquito** 600 bps

**housefly** 300 bps

**wasp** 250 bps

**hoverfly** 120 bps

**ladybug** 90 bps

**dragonfly** 30 bps

**locust** 20 bps

# Jumpers

The vertical leap of some of the best jumpers in the insect world

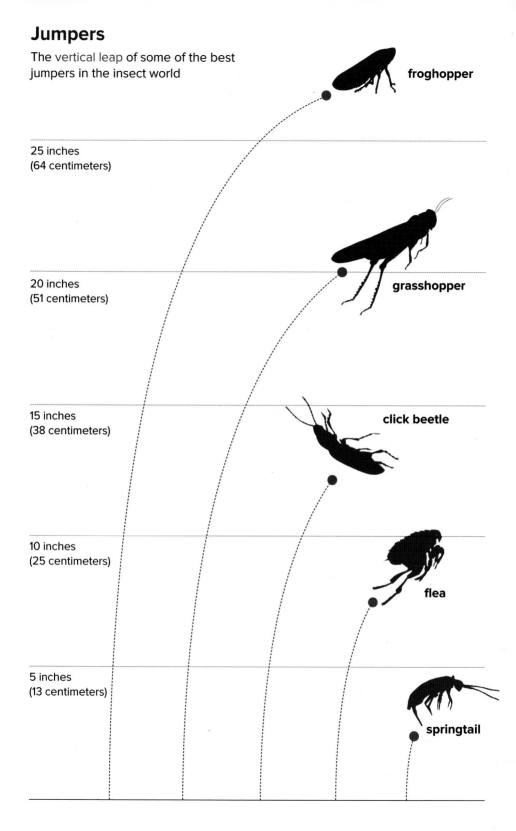

**froghopper**

25 inches
(64 centimeters)

20 inches
(51 centimeters)

**grasshopper**

15 inches
(38 centimeters)

**click beetle**

10 inches
(25 centimeters)

**flea**

5 inches
(13 centimeters)

**springtail**

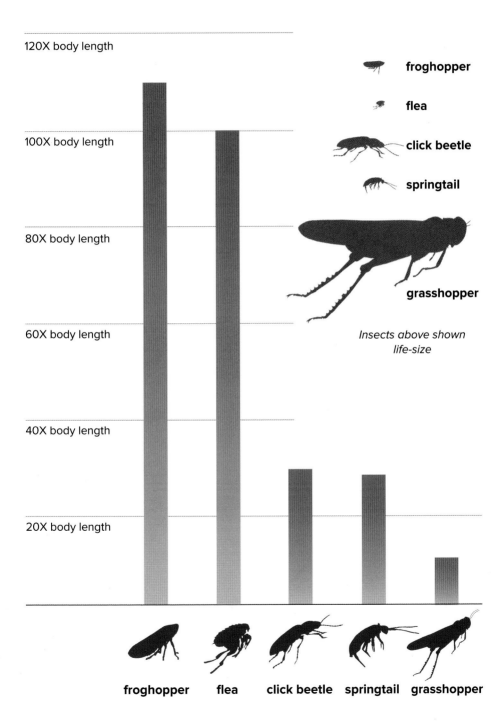

The height of an insect's jump compared to its body length

120X body length

100X body length

80X body length

60X body length

40X body length

20X body length

froghopper

flea

click beetle

springtail

grasshopper

*Insects above shown life-size*

froghopper   flea   click beetle   springtail   grasshopper

# Ouch!

Many insects defend themselves with a venomous sting. A scientist named Justin Schmidt created the **Schmidt Sting Pain Index**. It uses a scale of 1 to 4 to rate the pain of insect stings.

| **Sting Pain Index: 1** | **Sting Pain Index: 2** |
|---|---|
| *Slight pain, lasts only a few minutes.* | *Hot, searing pain. Lasts for up to ten minutes.* |

**sweat bee**

**honeybee**

actual size

actual size

Other insects with Level 1 stings

Other insects with Level 2 stings

**twig ant**    **western paper wasp**

**trap-jaw ant**    **yellow jacket**

*These insects are shown life-size.*

In his work as an entomologist—a scientist who studies insects—Justin Schmidt was stung by more than 100 different kinds of bees, wasps, and ants.

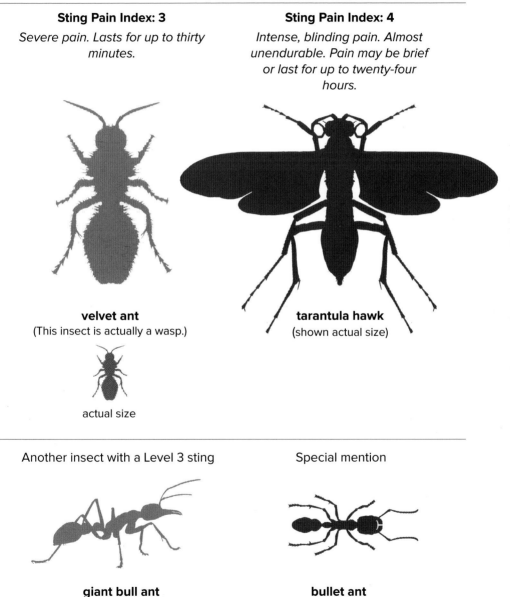

**Sting Pain Index: 3**

*Severe pain. Lasts for up to thirty minutes.*

**velvet ant**
(This insect is actually a wasp.)

actual size

**Sting Pain Index: 4**

*Intense, blinding pain. Almost unendurable. Pain may be brief or last for up to twenty-four hours.*

**tarantula hawk**
(shown actual size)

Another insect with a Level 3 sting

**giant bull ant**

Special mention

**bullet ant**
This ant gets a 4+ on the Sting Pain Index. The sting of this ant is said to feel like getting shot.

# Deadly insects

The size of each circle represents the estimated number of humans killed by insects each year.

**tsetse fly**
10,000 deaths

**fire ant**
30 deaths

**assassin bug**
12,000 deaths

**Japanese giant hornet**
40 deaths

**bee**
100 deaths

**sandfly**
24,000 deaths

## Cause of death

venom or allergic reaction

deadly disease carried by insect

**mosquito**
1,000,000 deaths

# The insect life cycle

Most insects go through several life stages. This process is called metamorphosis.

**The life cycle of the ladybird beetle, or ladybug**

A female ladybug lays about 50 eggs at a time.

Ladybug eggs take five to seven days to hatch.

The adult stage of the ladybug. These beetles can live for a year or more.

Ladybugs hibernate during the winter. They often cluster together in groups that include thousands of beetles.

The larva of a Hercules beetle, one of the largest insects

A larva hatches from the egg. After about three weeks, it will become . . .

Many insect larvae, including the ladybug's, go through several stages as they grow.

. . . a pupa. In about two weeks, it will become an adult beetle.

A butterfly pupa is called a chrysalis.

# Insect lifespans

Some insects live for just a day or two.
Others can survive for many years.

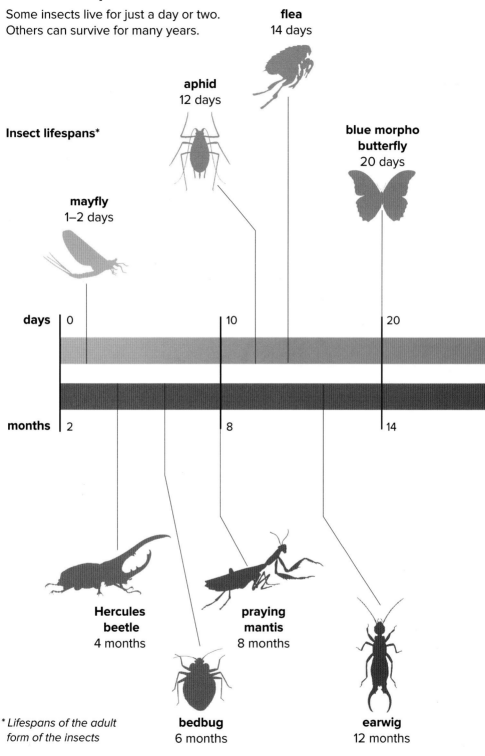

**flea**
14 days

**aphid**
12 days

Insect lifespans*

**blue morpho
butterfly**
20 days

**mayfly**
1–2 days

days | 0     10     20

months | 2     8     14

**Hercules
beetle**
4 months

**praying
mantis**
8 months

*Lifespans of the adult
form of the insects*

**bedbug**
6 months

**earwig**
12 months

24

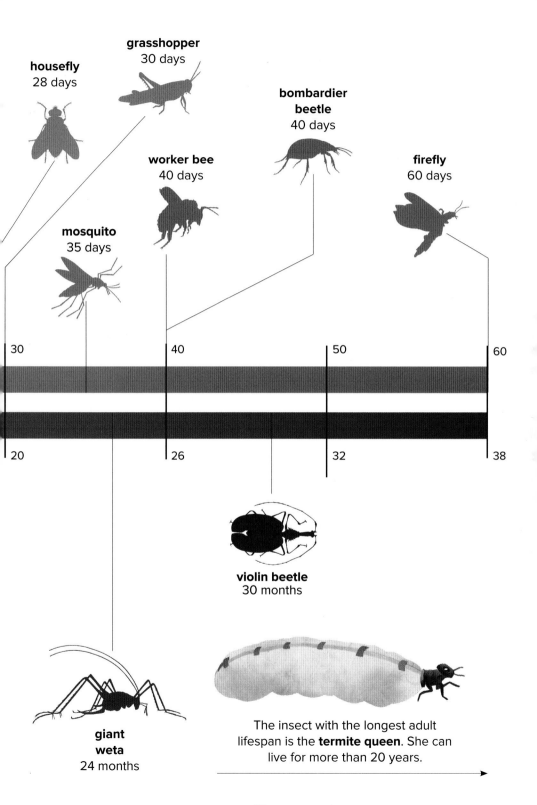

**housefly**
28 days

**grasshopper**
30 days

**bombardier beetle**
40 days

**worker bee**
40 days

**firefly**
60 days

**mosquito**
35 days

30    40    50    60

20    26    32    38

**violin beetle**
30 months

**giant weta**
24 months

The insect with the longest adult lifespan is the **termite queen**. She can live for more than 20 years.

# Insect vision

Insect eyes are made up of many individual lenses. They are called compound eyes.

The **dragonfly** can almost see in a complete circle.

The compound eyes of the **walking stick insect** are enormous.

A flower as we see it (top) and as a **bee** might see it (bottom)

Some insects, such as the **rove beetle**, have extra eyes. They are simple and probably serve to detect light.

# Glowing insects

A few insects are bioluminescent—
they produce their own light.

The **glowworm** is the
larva of a fungus gnat.
It lives in caves in
New Zealand, where
it dangles sticky
glowing threads to
capture flies.

The **railroad worm**
is a beetle larva.
It glows to warn
predators that it is
poisonous.

This **click beetle**
glows to attract the
flying insects it eats.

On warm summer
evenings, the **firefly**
flashes on and off to
attract a mate.

**Fireflies** are also
called **lightning bugs**.

# Noisy insects

To attract a mate, these insects make surprisingly loud sounds.

*These insects are shown life-size.*

The shape of the mole cricket's burrow makes its call louder.

**mole cricket**
The mole cricket rubs its wings against its legs to make a sound.

**water boatman**
The loudest animal on Earth for its size

**cicada**
The loudest insect humans can hear

**katydid**
The sound it makes is too high-pitched for human ears to hear.

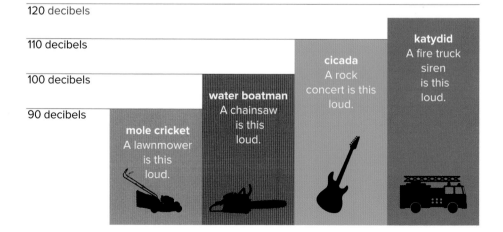

120 decibels

110 decibels

100 decibels

90 decibels

**katydid**
A fire truck siren is this loud.

**cicada**
A rock concert is this loud.

**water boatman**
A chainsaw is this loud.

**mole cricket**
A lawnmower is this loud.

# Insect ears

Most insects are deaf. The ones that can hear have ears on different parts of their body.

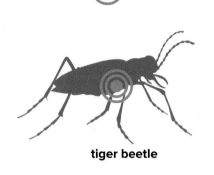 insect ear location

**scarab beetle**

**tiger beetle**

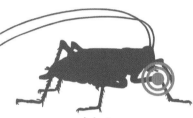

**cricket**

**hawk moth**

**praying mantis**

**water boatman**

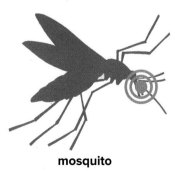

**mosquito**

**locust**

*These insects are not shown at actual size.*

# Insect builders

Many insects that live in colonies construct impressive nests.

**paper wasps**
Their nest is made of chewed-up wood pulp—a kind of paper.

**mound-building termites**
They build towering nests made of mud and saliva.

**How many insects live in a nest?**

800

2,000,000

**fire ant**
A pile of earth is formed as the ants dig out underground tunnels and chambers.

**Africanized bees**
These dangerous insects are also known as "killer bees." Their nests, or hives, can be attached to trees, rocks, or buildings.

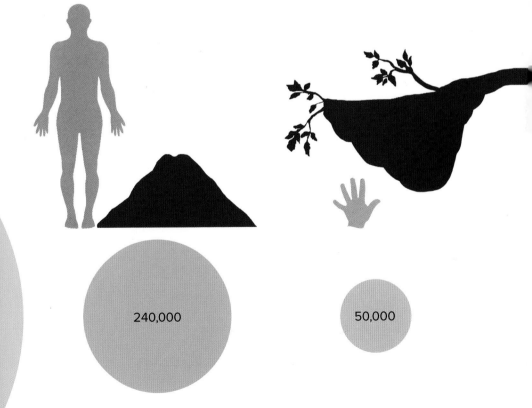

240,000

50,000

# Finding home

Desert ants live where the ground gets hot enough to kill many insects. The ants, which can survive high temperatures, feed on these dead insects. But they need to get home quickly so the heat doesn't kill them as well.

The ant wanders back and forth as it searches for food.

As soon as it finds a dead insect or other food, the ant heads directly back to its nest.

The desert ant uses visual landmarks, such as these rocks, to help it navigate.

The ant also keeps track of the number of steps it has taken on each part of its journey.

# Mosquito senses

A mosquito has several ways of finding a human to bite. Each method works at a different distance.

**1**
The mosquito detects the human's breath.

**2**
The mosquito sees its victim.

**3**
The mosquito detects the skin's odor.

**4**
The mosquito senses the body's heat.

**5**
Time for a tasty meal of blood!

# Insect migration

Some insects travel thousands of miles to find food, water, or a warm climate.

**monarch butterfly** ————

**locust** ————

**painted lady butterfly** ————

**globe skimmer dragonfly** ————

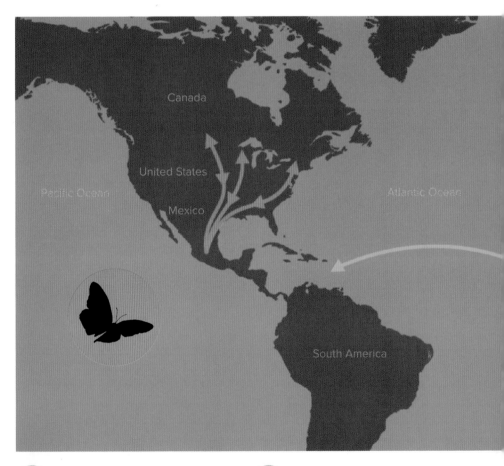

The **monarch butterfly** flies south to Mexico in the winter and heads north in the spring. A single butterfly can't make the whole trip in its lifetime. It can take four generations of monarchs to complete the journey.

**Locusts** migrate to find food, moving with the wind. In 1988, a swarm of locusts crossed the Atlantic Ocean.

| 2,000 mi.<br>(3,219 km.) | 4,000 mi.<br>(6,437 km.) | 6,000 mi.<br>(9,656 km.) | 8,000 mi.<br>(12,874 km.) | 10,000 mi.<br>(16,093 km.) | 12,000 mi.<br>(19,312 km.) |
|---|---|---|---|---|---|

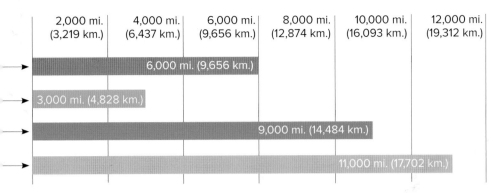

6,000 mi. (9,656 km.)

3,000 mi. (4,828 km.)

9,000 mi. (14,484 km.)

11,000 mi. (17,702 km.)

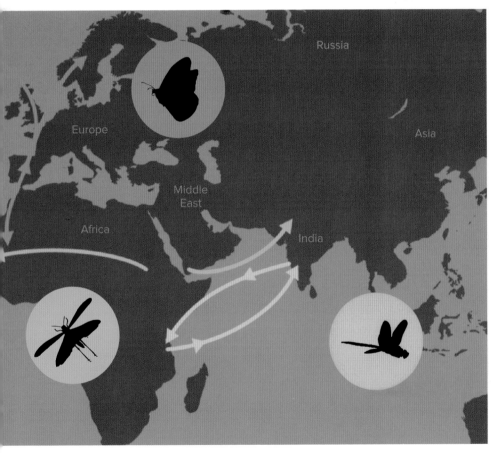

The **painted lady butterfly** stays warm during the winter in Africa. Its descendants return to northern Europe in the spring. It can take six generations of butterflies to make the round trip.

The record for longest insect migration is held by the **globe skimmer dragonfly**. It makes a round trip from Africa to India and back, following seasonal rains.

# Insect extremes

life-size

### Highest insect

A colony of **bumblebees** was found at an elevation of 18,400 feet (5,608 meters) on Mount Everest.

### Deepest insect

A tiny **midge**—a kind of fly—was discovered in a cave in Europe. It was living 3,215 feet (980 meters) below the surface.

 life-size

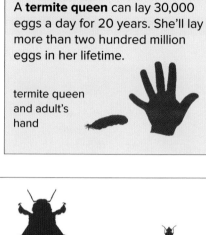

### The most eggs

A **termite queen** can lay 30,000 eggs a day for 20 years. She'll lay more than two hundred million eggs in her lifetime.

termite queen and adult's hand

---

### Largest and smallest eggs

The largest insect egg is that of the **carpenter bee**. A **parasitic fly** lays the smallest egg. It's too tiny to see with the naked eye.

carpenter bee and egg

The parasitic fly egg is too small to see.

---

**Fastest insect on land** The **Australian tiger beetle** can run at more than 5½ miles per hour (9 kilometers per hour).

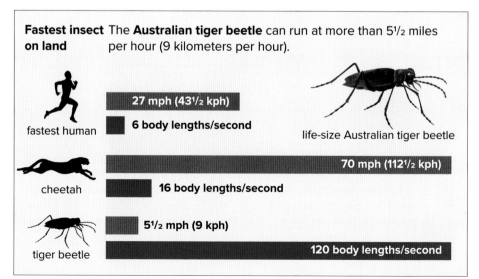

fastest human

27 mph (43½ kph)

6 body lengths/second

life-size Australian tiger beetle

cheetah

70 mph (112½ kph)

16 body lengths/second

tiger beetle

5½ mph (9 kph)

120 body lengths/second

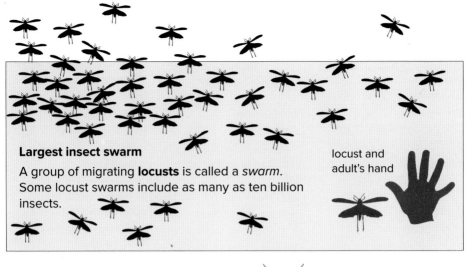

## Largest insect swarm

A group of migrating **locusts** is called a *swarm*. Some locust swarms include as many as ten billion insects.

locust and adult's hand

life-size

## Deadliest venom

A **harvester ant** has the most potent venom in the insect world. Eight hundred stings from these ants could kill an adult human.

## Longest life cycle

Before emerging as an adult, a **woodboring beetle** larva may spend more than 25 years inside a piece of wood.

life-size

## Temperature extremes

The **desert ant** can survive temperatures of 158°F (70°C). The larva of the **Antarctic midge** lives on the snow at temperatures as low as −4°F (−20°C).

158°F (70°C)

160°F (71°C)

140°F (60°C)

120°F (49°C)

100°F (38°C)

**desert ant** and **Antarctic midge** larva shown life-size

80°F (27°C)

60°F (16°C)

40°F (4°C)

32°F (0°C)

20°F (−7°C)

0°F (−18°C)

−4°F (−20°C)

−20°F (−29°C)

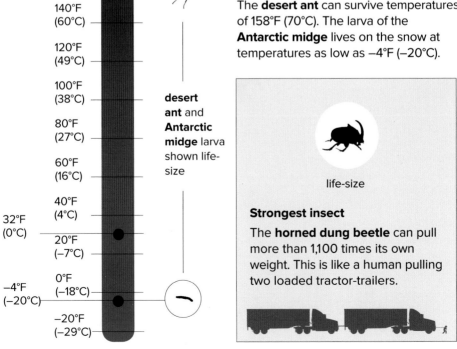

life-size

## Strongest insect

The **horned dung beetle** can pull more than 1,100 times its own weight. This is like a human pulling two loaded tractor-trailers.

# Glossary

**abdomen**
The third body segment of an insect. It contains the heart and digestive organs.

**allergic reaction**
The body's reaction to foreign substances. Sometimes the body's immune system overreacts, which can be harmful.

**antennae**
A pair of sense organs on or near the head of an insect. They are usually long, thin projections and are sometimes called "feelers."

**chrysalis**
The hard-shelled pupa of a butterfly—the stage of metamorphosis between caterpillar and adult.

**compound eyes**
Eyes found in insects and other arthropods. They contain many individual segments, each of which forms part of an image.

**decibel**
A unit used to describe the intensity of sound. A 10 decibel increase equals a sound that is ten times more intense.

**descendant**
An organism that is related to ancestors that lived in the past.

**generation**
All the individuals born at about the same time. Grandparents, parents, and children represent three different generations.

**hibernate**
To spend the winter asleep or in a resting state.

**hive**
The home or nest of some kinds of insects that live in colonies, including bees and wasps.

**infographics**
Facts and information presented visually as diagrams, charts, and graphs rather than just text.

**larva**
An immature form of an insect. Typically, larvae hatch from eggs. Caterpillars are the larvae of butterflies and moths.

**metamorphosis**
In insects, the process of changing form in a series of distinct stages as time passes.

**navigate**
To intentionally travel from one place to another using memory, landmarks, smells, or astronomical guides such as the Sun, Moon, and stars.

**potent**
Strong, powerful.

**pupa**
One of the stages of metamorphosis in many insects. Larvae become pupae, which will finally turn into adults.

**round trip**
A journey and a return to where the trip began.

**saliva**
A fluid created in the mouths of animals. Sometimes called "spit."

**species**
A group of living things that look alike, behave in a similar way, and are able to produce offspring.

**thorax**
The second body segment of an insect. It lies between the head and the abdomen. An insect's legs and wings are attached to its thorax.

**venomous**
The ability of an insect or other animal to inject venom with teeth, spines, or stingers.

**vertical leap**
The height of a jump measured from the ground to its highest point.

# Bibliography

*The Anatomy of Insects and Spiders.* By Claire Beverley and David Ponsonby. Chronicle Books, 2003.

*The Bees in Your Backyard: A Guide to North America's Bees.* By Joseph S. Wilson and Olivia J. Messinger Carril. Princeton University Press, 2015.

*Buzz: The Intimate Bond Between Humans and Insects.* By Josie Glausiusz. Chronicle Books, 2004.

*Extreme Bugs.* By Leslie Mertz. Harper Collins, 2007.

*Eyewitness Books: Insect.* By Laurence Mound. Alfred A. Knopf, 1990.

*Incredible Bugs.* By Rick Imes. Macmillan Canada, 1997.

*Innumerable Insects: The Story of the Most Diverse and Myriad Animals on Earth.* By Michael S. Engel. Sterling, 2018.

*An Inordinate Fondness for Beetles.* By Arthur V. Evans and Charles L. Bellamy. University of California Press, 2000.

*Ultimate Bugopedia.* By Darlyne Murawski and Nancy Honovich. National Geographic Children's Books, 2013.

longhorn beetle

**For Zoe**

hmhbooks.com

The illustrations are cut- and torn-paper collage.
The infographics are cut-paper silhouettes and graphics created digitally.
The text type was set in Proxima Nova.
The display type was set in Berthold Akzidenz Grotesk.

ISBN: 978-1-328-85099-7 hardcover
ISBN: 978-1-328-85100-0 paperback

Manufactured in China
SCP 10 9 8 7 6 5 4 3 2 1
4500794432